Boy ☠ STUFF

paper planes

FOLD THEM · THROW THEM · FLY THEM · CRASH 'EM!

PaRragon

Bath · New York · Singapore · Hong Kong · Cologne · Delhi
Melbourne · Amsterdam · Johannesburg · Shenzhen

Contents

paper planes

FOLD THEM • THROW THEM • FLY THEM • CRASH 'EM!

This edition published by Parragon, Inc. 2013

Parragon, Inc.
440 Park Avenue South, 13th Floor
New York, NY 10016

www.parragon.com

First published by Parragon Books Ltd. 2013

Copyright © Parragon Books Ltd 2013

Concept design and paper engineering by Creative Sweet
Images courtesy of Shutterstock.com

Written by Jason Loborik   Illustrated by David Semple and Creative Sweet
Edited by Michael Diggle   Designed by Alex Dimond
Production by Richard Wheeler

ISBN 978-1-4723-1831-2

Printed in China

Ready to make some awesome paper planes?

OKAY! HERE'S WHAT YOU'VE GOT ...

 A FOLDER WITH 3 USEFUL POCKETS. YOU CAN USE IT TO STORE STUFF IN!

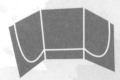 THIS BOOK, WHICH SHOWS YOU HOW TO MAKE YOUR PLANES.

 STICKERS FOR YOU TO CUSTOMIZE YOUR PLANES WITH!

A PAD OF FANTASTIC FLIGHT-READY PLANE DESIGNS!

HOW TO FOLD YOUR PAPER

EACH SHEET IN YOUR PAD HAS DOTTED LINES FOR YOU TO FOLD ALONG.

SOME SHEETS HAVE SOLID LINES AND A PICTURE OF SOME SCISSORS. CUT ALONG THE SOLID LINES.

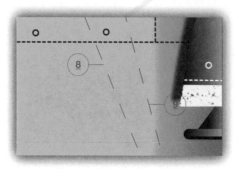

EACH FOLD LINE HAS A NUMBER NEXT TO IT. THIS NUMBER MATCHES THE NUMBER OF THE STEP-BY-STEP PICTURES IN THE BOOK. EASY, HUH? FOLLOW THE NUMBERS AND FOLD TO MATCH THE PICTURE.

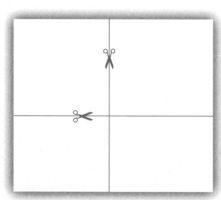

TOP TIPS

1. WHEN YOU SEE THIS SYMBOL, TURN YOUR PAPER OVER.  **FLIP IT!**

2. USE A RULER TO HELP YOU MAKE A STRAIGHT EDGE WITH LONGER FOLDS. PUT THE EDGE OF YOUR RULER ALONG THE DOTTED LINE AND FOLD THE PAPER OVER IT.

3. RUN YOUR FINGERNAIL ALONG THE TOP OF EACH FOLD TO MAKE SURE IT'S NEAT.

4. TRY TO FOLD EACH PLANE THE SAME ON BOTH SIDES (SYMMETRICALLY) TO HELP IT FLY BETTER.

5. MOST PLANES FLY BEST WHEN THE WINGS CURVE SLIGHTLY UPWARD AS SEEN FROM THE FRONT OF THE PLANE.

6. TRY ADDING A PAPER CLIP TO THE NOSE OF EACH PLANE TO SEE IF IT FLIES FARTHER.

7. IF YOUR PLANE DIVES TOO MUCH, BEND THE BACK OF THE WINGS UP SLIGHTLY.

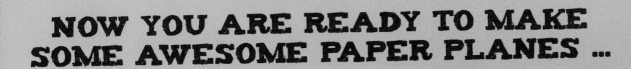

NOW YOU ARE READY TO MAKE SOME AWESOME PAPER PLANES ...

Let's go!

Jumbo Jet

THIS MIGHTY PLANE IS KING OF THE SKIES!

GET A PAIR OF SCISSORS READY. THIS WILL HELP YOU MAKE THE TAIL WING LIKE A PRO!

TEAR OUT YOUR JUMBO SHEET FROM THE PAD. START WITH THIS SIDE FACING YOU.

---

① FOLD THE PLANE IN HALF ALONG THE GUIDE.

② CUT ALONG THE GUIDE TO TAKE OUT THIS TRIANGLE PIECE.

③ FOLD ALONG THE GUIDE.

FLIP IT!

---

④ DO THE SAME FOLD AGAIN ON THE OTHER SIDE.

⑤ FOLD OVER TOWARD YOU. FOLD BACK THE OTHER WAY AND TUCK THE FLAP UNDERNEATH.

⑥ REPEAT ON THE OTHER SIDE.

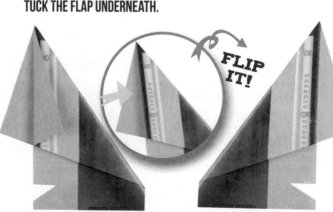

FLIP IT!

(7) FOLD DOWN THE FIRST SIDE OF THE JUMBO.

FLIP IT!

(8) REPEAT ON THE OTHER SIDE. THE WINGS ARE REALLY STARTING TO TAKE SHAPE NOW!

(9) FOLD UP THE FIRST WING.

FLIP IT!

(10) FOLD UP THE SECOND WING.

(11) OPEN UP THE MIDDLE OF THE PLANE AND FOLD UP THE TAIL OF YOUR JUMBO.

WHOA!

IS YOUR JUMBO READY TO GO? LET'S CHECK.

1. HOLD THE PLANE UP TO YOUR EYE AND LOOK ALONG THE WINGS.

2. MAKE SURE THE PLANE IS STRAIGHT AND THE WINGS ARE FOLDED LEVEL ON BOTH SIDES.

NOW I'M READY TO FLY THIS THING!

SPACE SHUTTLE

TEAR OUT THIS SHEET FROM THE PAD AND CUT ALONG THE GUIDE. KEEP THE TOP PIECE FOR THE ALIEN SPACESHIP ON PAGE 14.

YOU'RE GOING TO MAKE THE SHUTTLE FROM THE BOTTOM PIECE. START WITH YOUR PAPER LIKE THIS.

(1) FOLD IN HALF ALONG THE GUIDE.

(2) FOLD THE CORNER OVER. OPEN OUT YOUR PAPER A LITTLE AND FOLD THE TRIANGLE INSIDE.

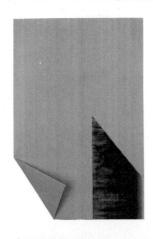

(3) FOLD ALONG THE GUIDE AND SEE THE WINGS START TO TAKE SHAPE.

10

④ FOLD UP THE EDGE ALONG THE GUIDE. FOLD BACK AND TUCK UNDERNEATH.

⑤ TURN YOUR PAPER OVER AND BEGIN THE SECOND WING BY FOLDING ALONG THE GUIDE.

FLIP IT!

⑥ FOLD UP THE EDGE ALONG THE GUIDE. FOLD BACK AND TUCK UNDERNEATH.

YOUR SHUTTLE SHOULD NOW LOOK LIKE THIS. TURN THE PAGE FOR THE FINISHING STEPS TO MAKE YOUR SHUTTLE AND **PREPARE TO LAUNCH!**

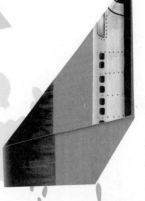

Q: WHY DID THE COW HITCH A RIDE IN A SPACE SHUTTLE?

A: IT WANTED TO SEE THE MOOOOOOOOOOOON!

11

THE MISSION CONTINUES ...

⑦ FOLD DOWN THE FIRST WING. TURN YOUR PAPER OVER. FOLD DOWN THE SECOND WING.

FLIP IT!

⑧ FOLD UP THE WING TIP. TURN YOUR PAPER OVER. FOLD UP THE SECOND WING TIP.

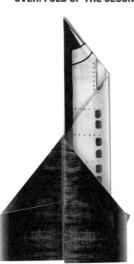

FLIP IT!

OPEN OUT YOUR SHUTTLE SO THAT IT LOOKS LIKE THIS FROM ABOVE.

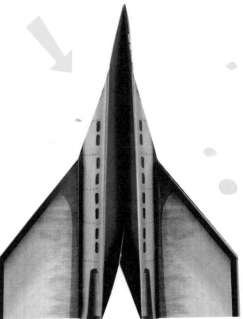

3 ... 2 ... 1 ...

BLAST OFF!

TRY IT!

YOU COULD LAUNCH YOUR SPACE SHUTTLE LIKE A NORMAL PAPER PLANE, BUT ISN'T THAT A BIT BORING?

INSTEAD, TRY LYING ON YOUR BACK AND SHOOT IT STRAIGHT UP INTO THE AIR TO SEE WHAT HAPPENS!

ALIEN SPACESHIP

THE ALIENS ARE COMING—TAKE COVER!

NOW YOU NEED THE TOP PIECE YOU CUT FROM THE SHEET ON PAGE 10. YOU KEPT IT NICE AND SAFE, RIGHT? GOOD!

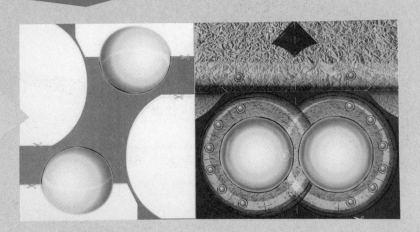

CUT THE PIECE IN HALF ALONG THE GUIDE. KEEP THE LEFT-HAND PIECE SAFE.

TAKE THE RIGHT-HAND PIECE—THIS WILL BECOME THE BASE OF YOUR ALIEN SPACESHIP.

① FOLD ALONG THE GUIDE.

FLIP IT!

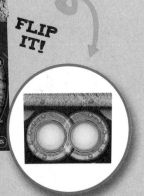

② FOLD IN HALF ALONG THE GUIDE.

③ FOLD THE CORNER OVER. OPEN OUT YOUR PAPER A LITTLE AND FOLD THE TRIANGLE INSIDE.

④ FOLD THE TOP LAYER OF THE CORNER ALONG THE GUIDE.

FLIP IT!

⑤ FOLD ALONG THE GUIDE.

⑥ FOLD THE TOP LAYER ALONG THE GUIDE.

⑦ TURN YOUR PAPER OVER AND REPEAT THE SAME FOLD ON THE OTHER SIDE.

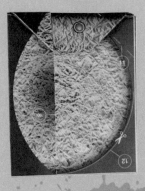

⑧ FOLD THE FIRST SIDE OF YOUR ALIEN SPACESHIP ALONG THE GUIDE.

FLIP IT!

YOUR SPACESHIP IS LOOKING GOOD, **EARTHLING!** TURN THE PAGE NOW TO FINISH YOUR CRAFT!

Q: HOW DO ALIENS KEEP THEMSELVES CLEAN?

A: THEY TAKE METEOR SHOWERS!

THE ALIEN ADVENTURE CONTINUES ...

(9) FOLD THE SECOND SIDE OF YOUR SPACESHIP ALONG THE GUIDE.

(10) OPEN OUT YOUR SPACESHIP LIKE THIS. FOLD THE LEFT CORNER ALONG THE GUIDE. OPEN OPEN OUT YOUR PAPER A LITTLE AND FOLD THE TRIANGLE INSIDE.

(11) REPEAT ON THE OTHER SIDE OF THE SPACESHIP.

(12) FOLD YOUR WINGS UP TOGETHER AND CUT ALONG THE GUIDE ON BOTH SIDES AT THE SAME TIME.

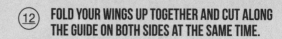

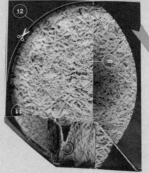

OPEN THE WINGS OUT AGAIN. THE BASE OF YOUR SPACESHIP IS NOW READY!

OKAY, NOW LET'S ADD A COCKPIT TO THE BASE SO THE ALIENS HAVE SOMEWHERE TO CONTROL THE SPACESHIP FROM.

TAKE THE OTHER PIECE OF PAPER.

CUT ALONG THE GUIDES. THERE ARE TWO BLUE COCKPITS TO MATCH YOUR ALIEN SPACECRAFT. THERE ARE ALSO TWO BLANK COCKPITS FOR YOU TO DRAW YOUR OWN ALIENS ON!

SLOT A COCKPIT INTO THE TOP OF YOUR SPACESHIP. SIMPLE, HUH?

TOP TIPS!

1. USE YOUR STICKERS TO ADD A FREAKY ALIEN PILOT TO YOUR COCKPIT.

2. TRY DRAWING YOUR OWN AWESOME ALIENS ON THE BLANK DOMES. MAKE THEM AS MEAN AND GREEN AS YOU LIKE!

3. IF YOUR COCKPIT FALLS OUT DURING FLIGHT, TRY ADDING A PAPER CLIP UNDERNEATH AT THE FRONT. THIS WILL HOLD YOUR SPACESHIP TOGETHER MORE TIGHTLY.

3-PLANE STACK

MAKE 'EM ALL FLY AT ONCE!

FIRST, PRACTICE THROWING THE SPACE SHUTTLE, ALIEN SPACESHIP, AND JUMBO JET.

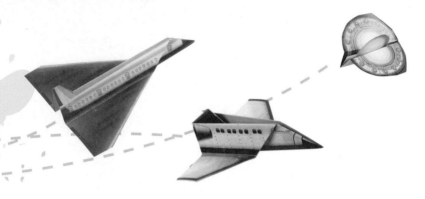

NEXT, TRY THROWING THE JUMBO JET WITH THE SPACE SHUTTLE TUCKED INTO THE TOP OF IT. THE TAIL WING OF YOUR JUMBO WILL HELP LAUNCH THE SHUTTLE.

READY TO TAKE IT TO THE NEXT LEVEL? TRY LAUNCHING ALL THREE AT ONCE!

GAME
PLANE CRAZY!

PLAY THIS GAME WITH A FRIEND TO SEE WHO'S
A FLYING ACE ... AND WHO'S A SAD CASE!

1. TAKE TURNS TO LAUNCH THE
3-PLANE STACK INTO THE AIR.

BEFORE THEIR THROW, EACH PLAYER
SHOULD GUESS WHICH OF THE THREE
PLANES WILL FLY THE FARTHEST.

2. WHEN THE PLANES HAVE LANDED, MARK
THE POSITION OF THE ONE THAT HAS FLOWN
THE FARTHEST.

3. WHOSE MARK IS FARTHEST AWAY FROM THE PLACE
WHERE THE PLANES WERE THROWN FROM? FOR EACH
ROUND OF THROWS, COUNT YOUR SCORES AS BELOW.

HOW TO SCORE

10 POINTS
THE PERSON WHOSE MARK IS FARTHEST
AWAY GETS 10 POINTS!

5 POINTS
EACH PLAYER GETS 5 POINTS IF THEY
CORRECTLY SAID WHICH PLANE WOULD
GO THE FARTHEST!

EACH PLAYER HAS THREE THROWS EACH.
THE PERSON WITH THE MOST POINTS
AT THE END IS THE WINNER—
YESSSSSS!

SUPERSONIC JET

IT'LL BREAK THE SOUND BARRIER

TEAR OUT THE SHEET FROM THE PAD.

THIS IS THE SIDE THAT NEEDS TO BE FACING YOU.

① FOLD IN HALF ALONG THE GUIDE.

OPEN YOUR PAPER OUT AGAIN.

FOLD UP YOUR JET AND GET READY TO GO SUPERSONIC! THAT'S FASTER THAN SOUND TRAVELS, DUDE!

② FOLD IN BOTH CORNERS TO THE RED DOT MARKED WITH A NUMBER 2.

③ FOLD IN BOTH SIDES TO THE RED DOT MARKED WITH A NUMBER 3.

④ FOLD BOTH SIDES TO THE MIDDLE ALONG THE GUIDES.

⑤ FOLD YOUR PLANE IN HALF.

FLIP IT!

FOLD OUT THE WINGS. NOW YOU'RE READY FOR TAKE-OFF!

BOOM

HOW FAST?

WHICH SHAPE OF PLANE DO YOU THINK IS BEST FOR SPEED? A THIN DARTLIKE PLANE LIKE THIS ONE, OR ANOTHER SHAPE? TEST EACH PLANE AS YOU MAKE IT.

Q: WHAT DO YOU CALL A FLYING POLICEMAN?
A: A HELI-COP-TER!

Stealth Plane

THE SHAPE AND DESIGN OF THIS PLANE MAKE IT HARD FOR ENEMY RADAR TO FIND. START WITH THE PAPER LIKE THIS.

① FOLD DIAGONALLY ALONG THE GUIDE AND OPEN THE SHEET OUT AGAIN.

② NOW FOLD ALONG THE OTHER DIAGONAL. OPEN THE SHEET OUT AGAIN.

FLIP IT!

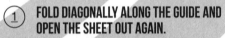

③ FOLD ALONG THE GUIDE AND OPEN THE SHEET OUT AGAIN.

④ FOLD THE SIDES MARKED WITH NUMBER 4 UPWARD AND INWARD TO MAKE A TRIANGLE SHAPE.

FLIP IT!

⑤ **FOLD OVER THE POINT OF THE TRIANGLE ALONG THE GUIDE.**

FLIP IT!

⑥ **FOLD IN HALF ALONG THE MIDDLE AND OPEN THE PLANE OUT AGAIN.**

⑦ **FOLD THE FIRST WING DOWN. TURN OVER AND FOLD THE SECOND WING DOWN.**

FLIP IT!

⑧ **OPEN OUT YOUR PLANE WITH THE UNDERSIDE TOWARD YOU. FOLD THE TOP LAYER ALONG THE GUIDES ON EACH SIDE.**

⑨ **FOLD ALONG THE GUIDES ON EACH SIDE. YOUR RADAR-JAMMERS ARE STARTING TO TAKE SHAPE!**

⑩ **FOLD ALONG THE GUIDES ON EACH SIDE TO COMPLETE YOUR RADAR-JAMMERS.**

FLIP IT!

⑪ **FOLD ALONG THE GUIDES ON EACH SIDE TO MAKE YOUR WING TIPS.**

NOW YOU'RE READY TO FLY UNDER THE RADAR!

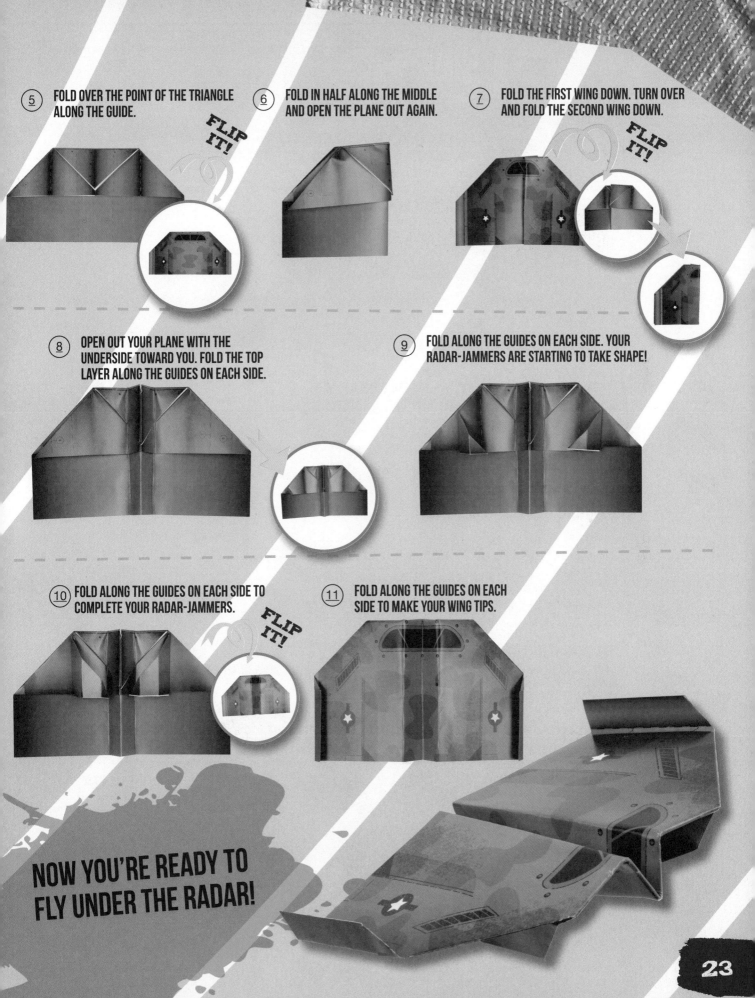

23

Jet P!ane

HERE'S THE SHEET YOU NEED. START OFF WITH IT FACING YOU LIKE THIS. OH, AND HAVE A PAIR OF SCISSORS READY, TOO!

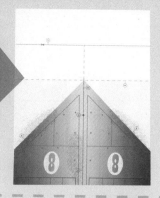

① SNIP OFF THIS STRIP WITH YOUR SCISSORS.

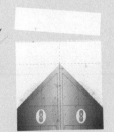

② FOLD ALONG THE GUIDE AND OPEN YOUR PAPER BACK OUT.

③ FOLD DOWN TOWARD YOU.

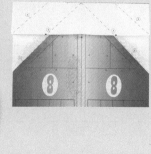

④ NOW TURN OVER THE TWO CORNERS TO THE RED DOTS MARKED WITH THE NUMBER 4.

⑤ MAKE TWO MORE FOLDS ALONG THE GUIDES TO SEE THE WINGS TAKE SHAPE.

FLIP IT!

Q: WHY DID THE BOY HAVE ALL HIS SCHOOL CLASSES IN AN AIRPLANE?

A: HE WANTED A HIGHER EDUCATION!

24

6. FOLD DOWN THE TIP TO THE RED DOT MARKED WITH THE NUMBER 6.

FLIP IT!

7. FOLD IN HALF ALONG THE GUIDE.

8. FOLD THIS TRIANGLE SHAPE ALONG THE GUIDE. OPEN THE FOLD BACK OUT.

9. FOLD ALONG THE GUIDE. TURN OVER AND REPEAT THE SAME FOLD ON THE OTHER SIDE.

FLIP IT!

10. OPEN OUT THE MIDDLE OF YOUR PLANE AND FOLD UP THE TAIL FIN.

TIME TO SEEK OUT ENEMY AIRCRAFT!

THUNDER FLAME

WATCH IT STORMING THROUGH THE SKIES!

IT'S PART-TUBE, PART-PLANE—BUT YOU WON'T BELIEVE HOW IT FLIES!

START WITH YOUR SHEET FACING YOU LIKE THIS.

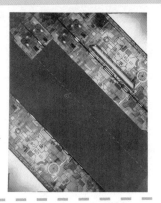

① FOLD ALONG THE GUIDE. MATCH THE BLUE AFTERBURNER FLAMES UP AT THE BOTTOM.

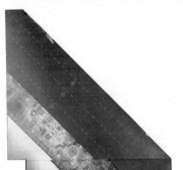

② FOLD ALONG THE GUIDE.

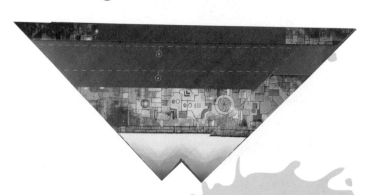

③ FOLD OVER AGAIN ALONG THE GUIDE.

④ FOLD OVER ONCE MORE ALONG THE GUIDE.

⑤ TURN THE PLANE OVER AND PUSH THE FOLDED SIDE ALONG THE EDGE OF A TABLE OR OTHER HARD SURFACE. THIS WILL GIVE YOU AN EVEN CURVE TO MAKE YOUR TUBE SHAPE.

FLIP IT!

(6) BRING UP THE POINTED ENDS OF THE LONG STRIP TO MAKE A TUBE SHAPE.

(7) TUCK EACH END INTO THE FOLD YOU MADE DURING STEP 4.

TOP TIPS!

WANT TO KNOW HOW TO MAKE THE THUNDER FLAME FLY?

HOLD IT LIKE THIS ...

... OR EVEN LIKE THIS. SEE WHICH WORKS BEST FOR YOU, AND WATCH IT STREAK THROUGH THE AIR LIKE A BOLT OF LIGHTNING!

MUTANT FLY

THINK THE THUNDER FLAME'S COOL? TRY MAKING YOUR OWN VERSION IN THE FORM OF A FREAKY FLY WITH FANGS!

YOU'LL NEED A RECTANGULAR PIECE OF PAPER ABOUT THE SAME SIZE AS THE THUNDER FLAME.

1. FOLLOW THE STEPS FOR FOLDING THE THUNDER FLAME UP TO NUMBER 4. YOU'LL FIND THIS ON PAGE 26.

2. DRAW SOME JAGGED TEETH ALONG THE FOLDED EDGE OF YOUR MUTANT FLY.

YOU COULD ALSO DRAW SOME MUTANT RIBS AND FOOD IN THE FLY'S DISGUSTING STOMACH!

FLIP IT!

3. DRAW MORE FEARSOME TEETH ALONG THE FOLDED EDGE ON THE OTHER SIDE OF YOUR MUTANT FLY.

DRAW A BODY, SCARY BUG EYES, AND WINGS.

28

④ FOLLOW STEPS 5 TO 7 FOR THE THUNDER FLAME ON PAGES 26 AND 27. YOU'LL FINISH WITH SOMETHING LIKE THIS.

Q: HOW DO YOU KEEP FLIES OUT OF THE KITCHEN?

A: STICK A HEAP OF MANURE IN THE LIVING ROOM!

FLY VS FLAME

HAVE YOU MADE THE THUNDER FLAME AND MUTANT FLY? AWESOME—NOW IT'S TIME TO CAUSE MAXIMUM MAYHEM!

1. STAND A FEW YARDS AWAY FROM A FRIEND.

2. LAUNCH YOUR PLANES AT THE SAME TIME AND SEE HOW LONG IT TAKES TO CAUSE AN IN-AIR COLLISION. IT'S TRICKIER THAN IT SOUNDS!

SAFETY ALERT! MAKE SURE YOU AND YOUR FRIEND AIM AWAY FROM EACH OTHER WHEN YOU THROW.

Butt Fart Plane

IS IT A FART, OR IS IT A PLANE?

ERM ... IT'S BOTH, ACTUALLY.

(1) GET YOUR SCISSORS AND CUT OFF A STRIP LIKE THIS. START WITH THE TOP PIECE.

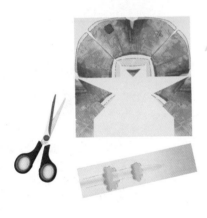

FLIP IT!

Q: WHAT HAS A BOTTOM AT ITS TOP?

A: A LEG!

(2) FOLD ALONG THE GUIDES AND OPEN THE SHEET OUT AGAIN EACH TIME.

FLIP IT!

③ FOLD THE PAPER IN HALF
AND OPEN BACK OUT.

④ NOW PUSH THE SIDES MARKED WITH
THE NUMBER 4 UPWARD AND INWARD
TO MAKE A TRIANGLE SHAPE.

FLIP IT!

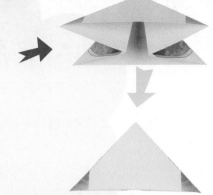

⑤ FOLD THE TOP LAYER ALONG THE
GUIDES ON EACH SIDE.

⑥ FOLD IN EACH SIDE AGAIN TO MAKE
A KITE SHAPE.

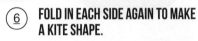

⑦ FOLD THE TOP OF THE KITE SHAPE DOWN
ALONG THE GUIDE.

⑧ TUCK IN THE FLAPS LIKE THIS.

I CAN REALLY
SEE THE BUTT TAKING SHAPE.
NOW, TURN OVER THE PAGE TO
ADD THE FART!

NOT MUCH FARTHER TO GO NOW!

⑨ TURN THE PAPER OVER AND FOLD ALONG THE GUIDE.

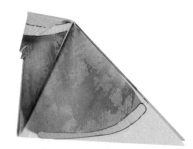

⑩ USE YOUR SCISSORS TO CUT ALONG THE GUIDE.

⑪ NOW IT'S TIME TO ADD THE FART BLAST! FOLD ALONG THE GUIDE AND OPEN THE PAPER BACK OUT.

SLOT INTO THE BACK OF YOUR BUTT AND YOU'RE READY TO FART AND FLY!

Q: WHY COULDN'T THE SKELETON FART?

A: BECAUSE IT DIDN'T HAVE THE GUTS!

PARRRRRRP!

FRRUPPP!

HA HA!

CAN YOU THINK OF ANY OTHER FUNNY NAMES FOR YOUR BUTT FART PLANE?

HOW ABOUT A **JUMBO BUTT?**

Q. WHAT HAPPENED TO THE SCIENTIST WHO INVENTED A FART-POWERED PLANE?

A. IT MADE HIM STINKING RICH!

CLASSIC PLANE

TEAR OUT THE CLASSIC PLANE FROM YOUR PAD, AND GRAB A PAIR OF SCISSORS TOO!

HERE'S WHAT TO DO ...

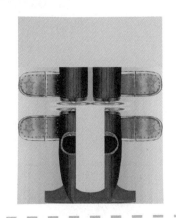

1. FOLD IN HALF ALONG THE GUIDE.

2. CUT OUT THE CURVED SHAPE ALONG THE GUIDE.

3. USE SCISSORS TO CUT ALONG THE GUIDE MARKED WITH A SOLID LINE. BE CAREFUL NOT TO CUT FARTHER THAN THE SOLID LINE!

4. OPEN THE PLANE OUT LIKE THIS IN FRONT OF YOU. NOW, FOLD ALONG THE GUIDE TOWARD YOU AND REPEAT AS SHOWN.

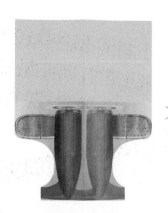

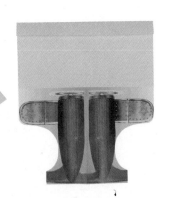

5.

6.

7.

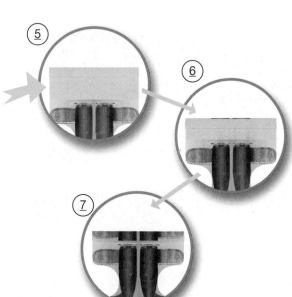

(8) FOLD ALONG THE GUIDE. YOUR PLANE WILL NOW LOOK LIKE THIS.

FLIP IT!

(9) FOLD IN HALF ALONG THE GUIDE.

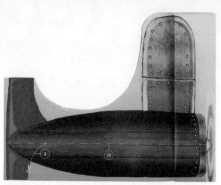

(10) FOLD THE FIRST WING DOWN ALONG THE GUIDE.

FLIP IT!

FOLD DOWN THE SECOND WING.

(11) OPEN OUT YOUR PLANE A LITTLE AND FOLD UP THE TAIL WING.

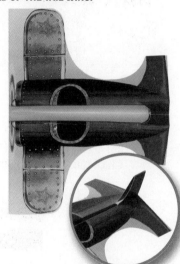

TRY IT!

TRY ADJUSTING THE WINGS OF YOUR CLASSIC PLANE BY BENDING THEM SLIGHTLY.

PRACTICE EXTREME DIVES, CLIMBS, AND CRAZY LOOP-THE-LOOPS!

MAKE SOME NOISY PLANE SOUND EFFECTS AS YOU THROW—BUT ONLY IF NO ONE IS WATCHING!

Rocket Wing

YOU'LL NEED YOUR SCISSORS FOR THIS FLAT-WING PLANE. IT'S A SIMPLE ONE TO MAKE, BUT IT'S AN ACE FLYER. IN FACT, YOU COULD SAY IT GOES LIKE A ROCKET!

① CUT ALONG THE SOLID LINES. KEEP YOUR TARGETS SAFE WHILE YOU FOLD YOUR ROCKET WING.

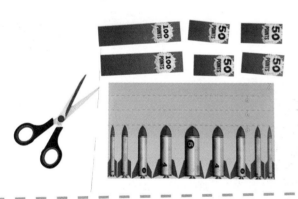

② FOLD ALONG THE GUIDE.

③ FOLD OVER AGAIN ALONG THE GUIDE.

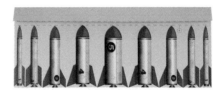

④ THIS FINAL FOLD ALONG THE GUIDE FINISHES THE FRONT OF YOUR ROCKET WING.

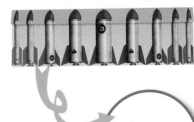

FLIP IT!

36

(5) FOLD IN HALF ALONG THE GUIDE. OPEN THE WING BACK OUT.

(6) FOLD UP THE EDGES OF THE WINGS.

TRY THIS!

TO FLY THIS PLANE, HOLD IT AT THE BACK BETWEEEN YOUR FINGERTIPS, THEN PUSH FORWARD WITH A SMOOTH MOTION AND LET GO.

Q: HOW DID THE ROCKET LOSE ITS JOB?

A: IT WAS FIRED!

TEST YOUR FLYING SKILLS ON THE NEXT PAGE!

BEE SWARM

IT'S THE PLANE THAT FLOATS LIKE A BUTTERFLY AND STINGS LIKE A BEE!

IF YOU THINK THE ROCKET WING TOTALLY ROCKS, THEN WHY NOT GET BUZZ-Y AND MAKE ANOTHER VERSION? YOU'LL NEED A RECTANGULAR PIECE OF PAPER ABOUT THE SAME SIZE AS THE ROCKET WING.

1. FOLLOW THE STEPS UP TO NUMBER 4 FOR FOLDING THE ROCKET WING ON PAGE 36.

2. NOW DRAW LOTS OF BEES IN A SWARM ALL OVER BOTH SIDES OF YOUR FOLDED PLANE, LIKE THIS ...

3. ... AND THIS.

FLIP IT!

4. FOLLOW STEPS 5 AND 6 FOR THE ROCKET WING ON PAGE 37. YOU'LL END UP WITH SOMETHING LIKE THIS.

BEE-HIVE YOURSELF AND MAKE ONE NOW!

ZOMBIE KNOCKDOWN

HERE'S A GAME TO PLAY WITH A FRIEND!

1. ONE PERSON HAS THE ROCKET WING AND THE OTHER HAS THE BEE SWARM VERSION.

2. STAND THE ZOMBIE TARGETS UP IN A ROW, AS SHOWN.

3. EACH PLAYER STANDS THE SAME DISTANCE AWAY FROM THE TARGETS AND THEY TAKE IT IN TURNS TO TRY TO KNOCK THEM OVER.

4. COUNT UP THE SCORE SHOWN ON THE FLIP SIDE. AFTER 3 TURNS EACH, THE WINNER IS THE PERSON WITH THE HIGHEST SCORE!

FOLD YOUR ZOMBIE TARGETS IN HALF AND STAND THEM LIKE THIS.

WHEN YOU KNOCK THEM DOWN, COUNT UP YOUR SCORE.

BOOM ZOMBIE KNOCKDOWN!

Bird of prey

MAKE IT GLIDE. MAKE IT SWOOP!

START WITH THIS SHEET.

GET A PAIR OF SCISSORS AND SOME STICKY TAPE READY, TOO.

① CUT ALONG THE GUIDE TO SEPARATE THE BIRD AND PTERODACTYL. KEEP YOUR PTERODACTYL SAFE TO FOLD LATER.

② FOLD IN HALF ALONG THE GUIDE.

FLIP IT!

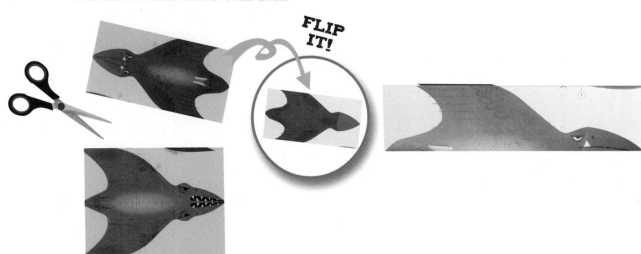

③ CUT OUT THE BIRD SHAPE CAREFULLY ALONG THE SOLID GUIDE LINE.

④ FOLD DOWN THE FIRST WING. TURN THE BIRD OVER, AND FOLD DOWN THE SECOND WING.

FLIP IT!

⑤ ATTACH A LITTLE PIECE OF TAPE ACROSS THE TAIL AND BEAK OF YOUR BIRD TO HOLD IT TOGETHER IN FLIGHT.

Q: WHAT DID THE LITTLE BIRD SAY TO THE BIG BIRD?

A: PECK ON SOMEONE YOUR OWN SIZE!

SQUAWK!

TOP TIPS!

ATTACH A PAPER CLIP TO THE NOSE OF YOUR BIRD TO HELP IT FLY FARTHER.

DRAW A SLIMY, WRIGGLY WORM OR TASTY BUG ON SOME OF THE PAPER YOU CUT OFF EARLIER. ATTACH IT TO YOUR BIRD'S BEAK WITH THE PAPER CLIP!

pterodactyl

MAKE YOUR FLYING BEAST WITH THE PIECE OF PAPER YOU KEPT SAFE ON PAGE 40.

YOU'LL NEED SCISSORS AND STICKY TAPE AGAIN.

①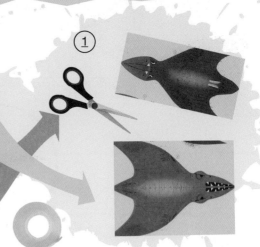

② FOLD IN HALF ALONG THE GUIDE.

③ CUT OUT THE PTERODACTYL SHAPE CAREFULLY ALONG THE SOLID GUIDE LINE.

④ FOLD DOWN THE FIRST WING. TURN YOUR PTERODACTYL OVER AND FOLD DOWN THE SECOND WING.

FLIP IT!

⑤ TURN UP THE EDGES OF THE WINGS ALONG THE GUIDES. ADD TAPE TO THE NOSE AND TAIL IN THE SAME WAY AS YOU DID FOR THE BIRD OF PREY ON PAGE 41.

SCREECH!

KLAKKKK!

TERROR-DACTYL!

SEE IF YOU CAN LAUNCH A TOTALLY TERRIFYING PTERODACTYL ATTACK IN MIDAIR!

GET SOME FRIENDS TO THROW PAPER PLANES IN FRONT OF YOU. LAUNCH YOUR PTERODACTYL AND SEE IF YOU CAN KNOCK ONE OF THEM TO THE GROUND IN A SINGLE SWOOP!

Q: WHY DID THE PTERODACTYL CROSS THE ROAD?

A: BECAUSE CHICKENS HADN'T EVOLVED YET!

SPACE ROCKET

IT'S OUT OF THIS WORLD!

ARE YOU READY TO LAUNCH A ROCKET ON AN INTERGALACTIC MISSION? START WITH THIS SHEET.

---

① FOLD IN HALF ALONG THE GUIDE AND OPEN OUT AGAIN.

② FOLD IN THE TWO CORNERS ALONG THE GUIDES TO THE RED DOT MARKED WITH A NUMBER 2.

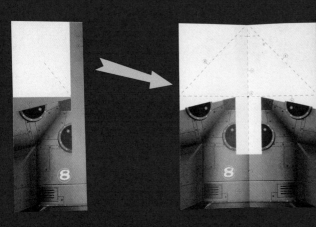

---

③ FOLD THIS TRIANGLE SHAPE ALONG THE GUIDE.

④ FOLD IN THE SIDES ALONG THE GUIDES TO THE RED DOT MARKED WITH A NUMBER 4.

⑤ FOLD ALONG THE GUIDE TO MAKE A SMALL TRIANGLE.

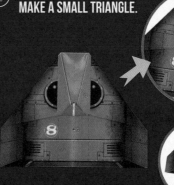

FLIP IT!

6. FOLD IN HALF ALONG THE GUIDE.

7. FOLD THE FIRST WING ALONG THE GUIDE. TURN YOUR ROCKET OVER AND FOLD DOWN THE SECOND WING.

FLIP IT!

8. FOLD YOUR ROCKET WINGS OUT LEVEL.

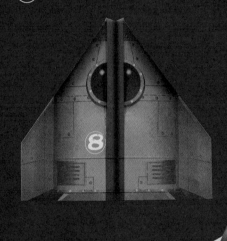

BUCKLE UP, ASTRONAUT!

IT'S TIME TO SHOOT FOR THE STARS.

Q: HOW DO YOU SEND A BABY ASTRONAUT TO SLEEP?

A: YOU ROCKET!

Rocket Robot

WHO SAYS ROBOTS CAN'T FLY?

MAKE A ROCKET ROBOT TO CHALLENGE THE FLYING POWER OF YOUR AWESOME SPACE ROCKET!

FIND A PIECE OF PAPER ABOUT THE SAME SIZE AS THE SPACE ROCKET TO GET STARTED.

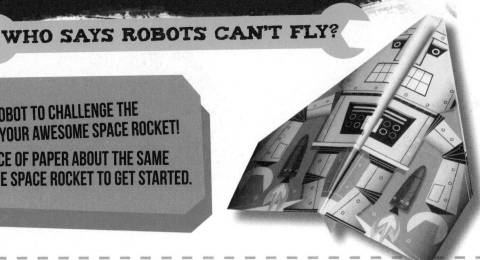

1. FOLLOW THE STEPS UP TO NUMBER 5 FOR HOW TO FOLD THE SPACE ROCKET. YOU'LL FIND THESE ON PAGE 44.

2. DRAW A MEGA ROCKET ROBOT ONTO YOUR PAPER LIKE THE ONE IN THIS PICTURE.

LEAVE A SPACE DOWN THE MIDDLE OF THE PAPER AS WIDE AS THE FLAT EDGE AT THE TOP.

THIS IS SO THAT BOTH SIDES OF YOUR ROBOT MATCH UP WHEN YOU FINISH FOLDING IT.

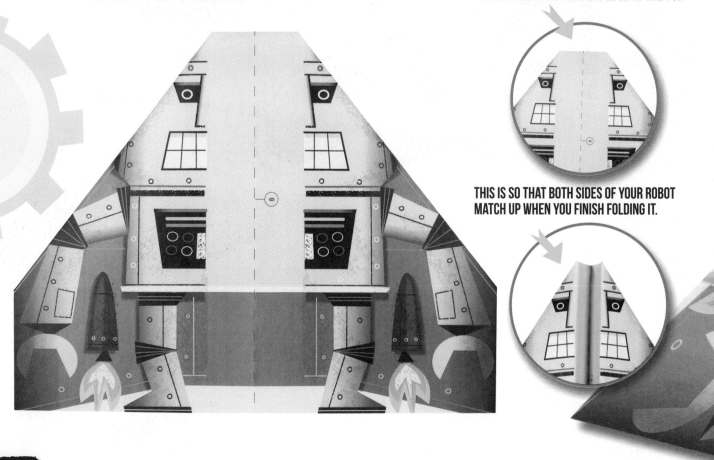

③ FOLLOW STEPS 6 TO 8 FOR FOLDING THE SPACE ROCKET ON PAGE 45. YOU COULD REPEAT YOUR ROBOT DESIGN ON THE OTHER SIDE OF THE WINGS AS YOU FOLD.

FOLD THE WINGS OUT SO THEY ARE LEVEL. NOW YOUR DROID IS READY TO LAUNCH!

Q: WHY WAS THE ROBOT ANGRY?

A: BECAUSE SOMEONE KEPT PUSHING ITS BUTTONS!

UFO Spinners

THEY'RE FREAK-TASTIC FLYING SAUCERS!

TO MAKE YOUR UFO SPINNERS, YOU'LL NEED SCISSORS, DRINKING STRAWS, AND STICKY TAPE ... NOT FORGETTING THIS SHEET FROM YOUR PAD!

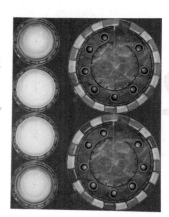

1. CUT OUT THE CIRCULAR SHAPES FROM THE SHEET.

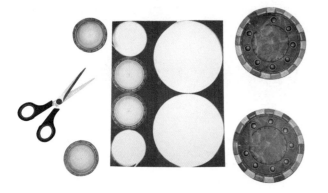

2. CUT OUT ALONG THE SOLID LINE TO THE CENTER. SNIP ALONG THE SMALL LINES WITHIN THE INNER CIRCLE.

3. OVERLAP THE PAPER ALONG THE LONG CUT TO THE DOTTED LINE. SECURE THE OVERLAP WITH STICKY TAPE. THIS WILL MAKE A CONE SHAPE.

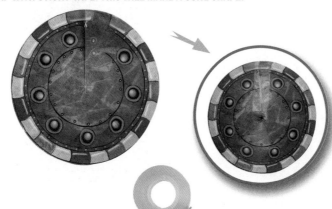

4 TAKE A DRINKING STRAW. CUT THE BENDY END OFF WITH A PAIR OF SCISSORS IF IT HAS ONE. MAKE FOUR CUTS INSIDE OF THE DRINKING STRAW. OPEN OUT THE ENDS.

POKE THE STRAW THROUGH THE HOLE IN THE SPINNER FROM UNDERNEATH.

STICK THE OPENED-OUT ENDS TO THE UNDERSIDE OF YOUR SPINNER.

YOUR SPINNER SHOULD NOW LOOK LIKE THIS.

GOOD SO FAR, BUT WHERE ARE THE ALIENS GONNA SIT TO FLY THE UFO?! IT'S TIME TO MAKE THE UFO COCKPIT.

UFO Spinners

5. CUT A TRIANGLE SHAPE FROM THE UFO DOME. SNIP ALONG THE SMALL LINES WITHIN THE INNER CIRCLE.

6. OVERLAP THE PAPER AS FAR AS THE DOTTED LINE TO MAKE ANOTHER CONE SHAPE. SECURE THE OVERLAP WITH STICKY TAPE.

7. FINALLY, PUSH THE DOME ONTO THE SAUCER SHAPE.

8. NOW, MAKE YOUR SECOND UFO SPINNER IN THE SAME WAY! USE YOUR STICKERS TO PUT SOME FREAKY ALIENS ON YOUR UFOs.

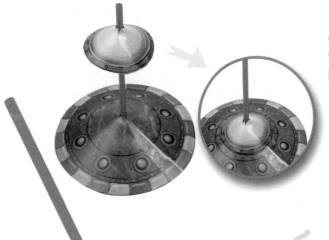

YOU COULD EVEN DRAW YOUR OWN ON THE BLANK EXTRA DOMES.

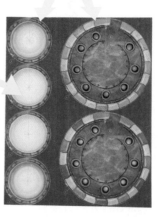

50

TOP TIP!

1. HOLD THE STRAW OF YOUR UFO SPINNER BETWEEN THE PALMS OF YOUR HANDS.

2. QUICKLY RUB ONE HAND ALONG THE OTHER AND LET GO ...

3. WATCH YOUR UFO SPIN OFF INTO THE ATMOSPHERE!

GET YOUR ZOMBIE TARGETS FROM PAGE 36 AND TRY ANOTHER KNOCKDOWN GAME USING YOUR UFO SPINNERS.

CAN YOU MASTER YOUR SPIN AND GET YOUR UFO ON TARGET?

YOU GOTTA SPIN TO WIN!

ALIEN INVADER

A SCARY SPACESHIP FROM ANOTHER WORLD!

YOU'LL NEED THIS SHEET FROM YOUR PAD. START OFF WITH IT FACING YOU AS SHOWN.

① FOLD ALONG THE GUIDE AND OPEN THE PAPER OUT AGAIN.

Q: WHAT DO YOU CALL AN ALIEN SPACESHIP THAT DRIPS WATER?

A: A CRYING SAUCER!

② FOLD ALONG THE GUIDE AND OPEN THE PAPER OUT AGAIN.

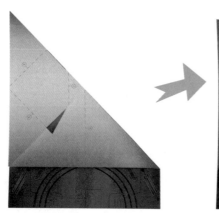 

FLIP IT!

③ FOLD OVER TOWARD YOU. OPEN THE PAPER OUT AND TURN IT OVER.

FLIP IT!

④ PUSH THE SIDES UPWARD AND INWARD AT THE POINTS MARKED TO MAKE A TRIANGLE SHAPE.

⑤ FOLD ALONG THE GUIDES TO MAKE A DIAMOND SHAPE.

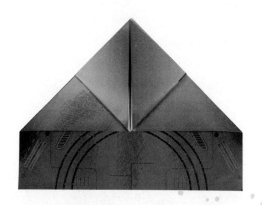

⑥ FOLD ALONG THE GUIDES. OPEN THE FOLDS OUT. FOLD BACK THE OTHER WAY AND TUCK THE FLAPS UNDERNEATH.

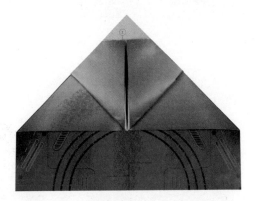
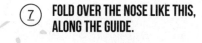

⑦ FOLD OVER THE NOSE LIKE THIS, ALONG THE GUIDE.

HEE HEE! I CAN MAKE TWO PLANES AT THE SAME TIME WITH MY FOUR ARMS!

ALIEN INVADER

COMPLETE YOUR CRAFT
AND GET READY TO INVADE ...

(8) TUCK BOTH CORNERS INTO THE FLAP.

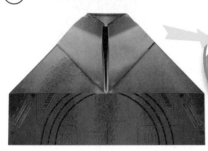  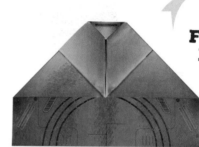

FLIP IT!

(9) FOLD ALONG THE GUIDES SO THAT EACH SIDE POINTS UP TOWARD YOU.

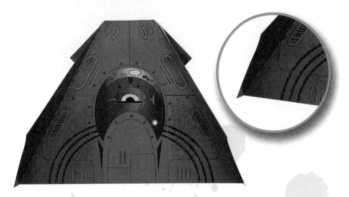

(10) FOLD OVER EACH WING TIP.

Q: WHAT DID THE ALIEN SAY TO THE FLOWER GARDEN?

A: TAKE ME TO YOUR WEEDER!

TOP TIPS!

FOR THE BEST FLYING RESULTS, HOLD THE ALIEN INVADER AT THE BACK, AS SHOWN. THEN PUSH FORWARD AND LET GO ... AND SEE IT SOAR THROUGH SPACE!

Hang Glider

THERE ARE A FEW STEPS INVOLVED WITH THIS PLANE, BUT DON'T WORRY, YOU'LL SOON GET THE **HANG** OF IT!

1. FOLD IN HALF ALONG THE GUIDE AND OPEN YOUR PAPER BACK OUT.

2. FOLD OVER THE CORNERS ALONG THE GUIDES TO THE RED DOT MARKED WITH THE NUMBER 2.

3. FOLD ALONG THE GUIDE.

4. FOLD EACH CORNER IN ALONG THE GUIDES TO THE RED DOT MARKED WITH THE NUMBER 4.

5. FOLD UP THE SMALL TRIANGLE ALONG THE GUIDE.

FLIP IT!

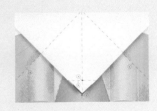

(6) FOLD IN HALF ALONG THE GUIDE.

(7) FOLD DOWN THE FIRST WING. TURN YOUR PAPER OVER AND FOLD DOWN THE SECOND WING.

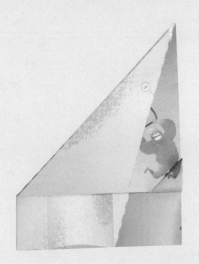

FLIP IT!

TOP TIP!

WANT TO MAKE YOUR HANG GLIDER SOAR? TRY ADDING A PAPER CLIP A LITTLE WAY BACK FROM THE NOSE OF THE PLANE ON THE UNDERSIDE. THIS WILL HELP BALANCE THE WEIGHT OF THE GLIDER IN FLIGHT.

OPEN OUT YOUR WINGS AND GET READY TO GLIDE.

SPY PLANE

IT'S ON A TOP-SECRET FLIGHT!

YOUR MISSION IS TO FOLD AND FLY YOUR OWN **SPY PLANE!**

① FOLD ALONG THE GUIDE AND OPEN YOUR PAPER OUT AGAIN.

② FOLD OVER THE CORNERS ALONG THE GUIDES.

③ FOLD OVER TOWARD YOU ALONG THE GUIDE.

FLIP IT!

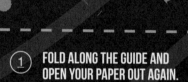

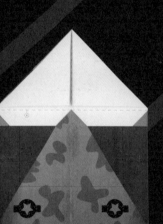

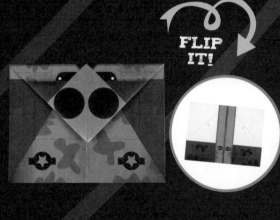

④ FOLD IN THE CORNERS ALONG THE GUIDES.

⑤ FOLD ALONG THE GUIDES. PART OF THE FOLD TUCKS UNDER THE TOP LAYER.

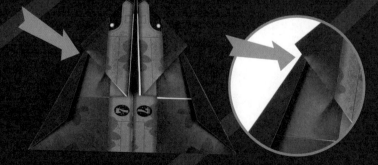

58

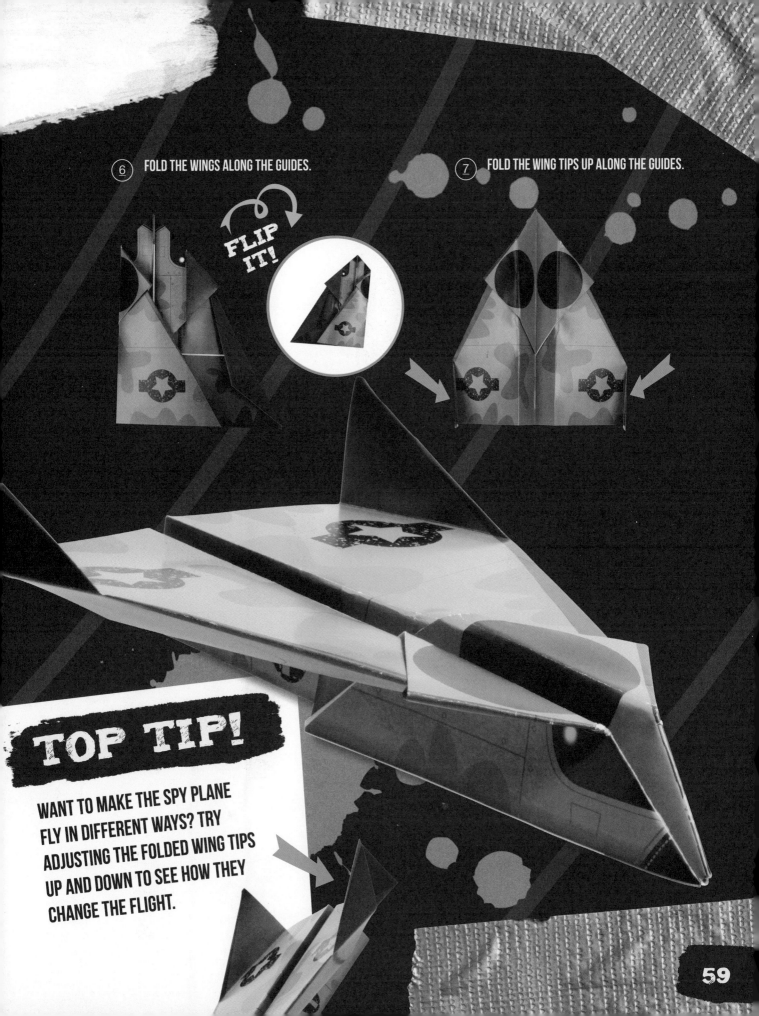

⑥ FOLD THE WINGS ALONG THE GUIDES.

FLIP IT!

⑦ FOLD THE WING TIPS UP ALONG THE GUIDES.

TOP TIP!

WANT TO MAKE THE SPY PLANE FLY IN DIFFERENT WAYS? TRY ADJUSTING THE FOLDED WING TIPS UP AND DOWN TO SEE HOW THEY CHANGE THE FLIGHT.

Spiral Spinners

YOU CAN MAKE FOUR SPIRAL SPINNERS FROM THIS SHEET!

CUT EACH ONE OUT AS A LONG STRIP, LIKE THIS, THEN FOLLOW THE STEPS BELOW TO MAKE EACH ONE.

(1) **CUT ALONG THE GUIDE.**

(2) **MAKE SMALL CUTS CAREFULLY ALONG THE GUIDES.**

(3) **FOLD ALONG THE GUIDES.**

(4) **FOLD THE BOTTOM PART UPWARD ALONG THE GUIDE.**

(5) **FOLD OVER THE BOTTOM CORNERS ALONG THE GUIDES. OPEN OUT THE FOLDS AND TUCK THE CORNERS INSIDE.**

6 CUT CAREFULLY ALONG THE GUIDES. TUCK THE FLAPS BEHIND THE FOLDS UNDERNEATH.

7 FOLD THE SPIRAL BLADES ALONG THE GUIDES. OPEN ONE BLADE OUT AND FOLD BACK THE OTHER WAY.

FLIP IT!

TOP TIPS!

1. HOLD YOUR SPIRAL SPINNER LIKE THIS.

2. PUT YOUR HAND UP IN THE AIR AS HIGH AS YOU CAN.

3. NOW LET GO! AS IT FALLS, THE BLADES WILL BEGIN TO SPIN LIKE A HELICOPTER—AWESOME!

TARGET GAME

1. MAKE YOUR SPIRAL SPINNERS AND THEN CHALLENGE SOME FRIENDS TO A TARGET COMPETITION. PICK A COLOR EACH.

2. FIRST, EITHER PLACE THIS BOOK FLAT ON THE FLOOR, OR COPY THE TARGET OPPOSITE ONTO A BIG SHEET OF PAPER.

3. EACH PLAYER TAKES A TURN TO DROP THEIR SPIRAL SPINNER ONTO THE TARGET FROM AS HIGH IN THE AIR AS THEY CAN REACH. WATCH VERY CAREFULLY TO SEE WHERE THE SPINNER HITS THE TARGET.

4. COUNT UP THE POINTS. THE PERSON WITH THE MOST POINTS AFTER 3 GOES IS THE WINNER!

25

50

25   50   100   50   25

50

25

63

SO, WHICH AWESOME PLANE FLIES THE BEST?

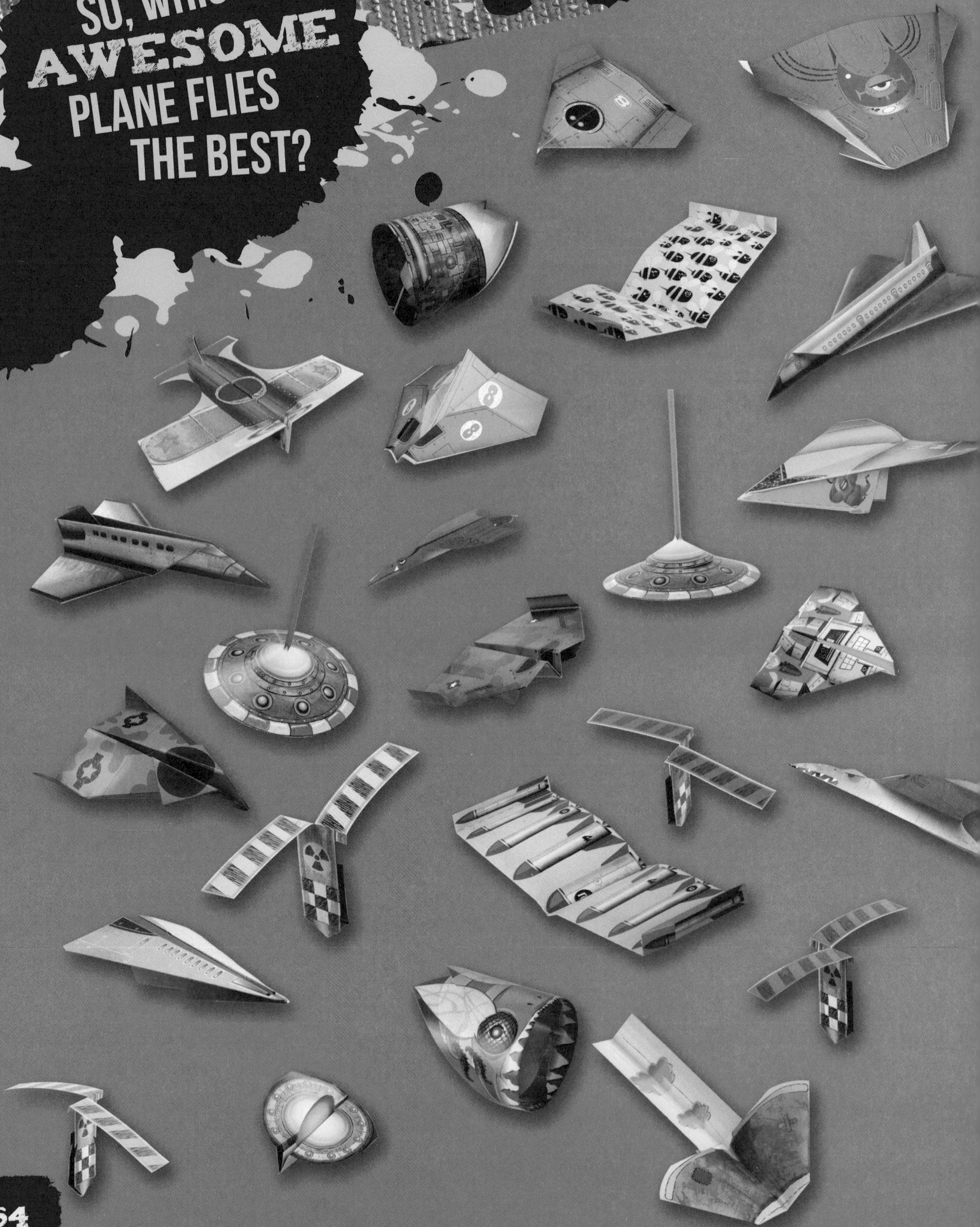